THOUGHTS FOR THE FREE LIFE

Lao Tsu to the Present

Cicely Buckley, Editor

Oyster River Press

Copyright © 1997, third edition, by
Cicely Buckley, editor and illustrator.

ISBN 1-882291-56-5

Translations from French and Spanish by
Cicely Buckley; from classical Chinese,
by Xiao-Ming Li and Peng Xu; from
the German, by Mechthilde Romoser.

Cover and drawings by Cicely
Calligraphy by Shou-Xian Ren and Kate Glanz.

*

Other books from the Oyster River Press:

Crow Milk. Poems by Rick Agran. 1997.
Edged in Light. Poems by Jane Jordan. 1993.
Halcyon Time. Poems on the birds by Hugh Hennedy.
   Inkbrush drawings by Charles Chu. 1993.
Intense Experience: Social Psychology through Poetry. Fred Samuels, Ed.
Is it Poison Ivy? By Joan Raysor Darlington, author & illustrator. 1993.
The Mending of the Sky and other Chinese Myths.
   Retold by Xiao Ming Li. Illustrations by Shean Ming Wu. 1989.
Paul Eluard: Ombres et Soleil~Shadows & Sun. Writings of 1913-1952.
   Illus. by Picasso, Magritte, Chagall, Andre Lhote. Translations by
   Cicely Buckley & Lloyd Alexander. 1995
Peace in Exile. Poems by David Oates. Cover & free-flow maps by
   Joan R. Darlington. 1992

Oyster River Press
20 Riverview Road, Durham, NH 03824

Much as I own I owe
The passers of the past,
Because their to and fro
Has cut this road to last . . . .

Robert Frost 1874-1963

Remembering Will Taylor 1894-1976

and

Phoebe Taylor 1895-1993

In midnight there is a budding morrow.

— John Keats

Acknowledgements

John F. Kennedy quotation is from remarks made at Amherst College, Oct. 26, 1963. Robert Kennedy quotation is from an address at the University of Capetown, South Africa, June 6, 1966.

Verses by Mahmoud Darwish are from *Selected Poems*, Ian Wedde and Fawwaz Tugan, translators. Copyright © by Ian Wedde, 1973. Reprinted by permission of Carcanet Press, Ltd.

American Indian wisdom is from *Nootka and Quileute Music* by Frances Densmore, ed., Bureau of American Ethnology, Bull. 124 (US Gov't Printing Office, 1939), p. 285. Quote from *Seven Arrows* by Hyemeyohsts Storm, p. 21. Copyright © by Hyemeyohsts Storm, 1972. Reprinted by permission of Harper & Row, Publishers, Inc. Quote from M.E.Gridley, *Contemporary American Indian Leaders*, 1972, p.138, reprinted by permission of Dodd, Mead & Co.

"Unidad" from *Residencia en la Tierra*, Copyright © 1973 by Pablo Neruda is reprinted by permission of New Directions Publishing Corporation.

Poem from *Later poems of Rabindranath Tagore,* Funk & Wagnalls, NY., 1976, copyright © 1974 by Peter Owen Ltd; translation copyright © by Aurobindo Bose. Reprinted by permission of Harper and Row Publishers, Inc.

Translation from *Paul Eluard: Ombres et Soleil ~Shadows and Sun: writings of 1913-1952,* Oyster River Press, copyright © 1995.

"Yes is a pleasant country" and "life is more true than reason will deceive", copyright 1944, © 1972, 1991 by the Trustees for the E. E. Cummings Trust; lines from "hate blows a bubble of despair into", copyright 1940, © 1968, 1991 by the Trustees for the E.E. Cummings Trust, from *Complete Poems: 1904-1962* by E. E. Cummings, edited by George J. Firmage. Reprinted by permission of Liveright Publishing Corporation.

Haiku by Kyoshi, translated by Sylvia Cassedy and Kunihiro Suitake, from *Birds, Frogs and Moonlight*, © 1967. Reprinted by permission of Doubleday & Co.

Sanskrit quotations from Paul Elmer More, *A Century of Indian Epigrams: chiefly from the Sanskrit of Bhartrihari* (Boston, Houghton Mifflin, 1899).

Yoruba sayings are in *Not Every God is Ripe Enough*, stories told by B. Gbadamosi and U. Beier, London, Ibadan & Nairobi: © Heinemann Educational Books Ltd and Ulli Beier, 1968.

Lines from *The Aeneid of Virgil, a verse translation*, VI 792, by Rolfe Humphries, are reprinted with permission of Macmillan Publishing Company. Copyright © 1987 by Macmillan Publishing Company.

Our heartfelt thanks to others who have generously given permission to quote from their works:

May Sarton wrote in 1992 with her permission for "Of Molluscs" and "Love" for this edition of *Thoughts*...

Jerome B. Seaton for translations of Feng Tzu-Chen and Yün K'an Tzu from *The Wine of Endless Life: Taoist Drinking Songs from the Yuan Dynasty*, 1978, Ardis Publishing, Ann Arbor, Mi.

Harlan Ellison for permission to reprint lines from his introduction to *Alone Against Tomorrow*, © copyright 1971, all rights reserved.

Illustrations on pages 23 and 98 are from a painting by Sesson (1504-1589) and on page 56, from a hand scroll by Zhou Chen (1500-1535), at the Freer Gallery of Art, Washington, D.C. Illustration on page 101 (a man in a house beneath a cliff) is from a brush painting by Tao-chi (1641-c.1717), in the Nü Wa Chai collection.

CONTENTS

Foreword   1

I.   Free Thought   7

II. The Natural Way   25

III. Life In Time   45

IV. Art of Living   75

V.   Out of Time   97

Index of Authors
and Original Languages   108

FOREWORD

The present edition with its wisdom from many cultures has been expanded with important ideas from Wordsworth, Henry David Thoreau, e. e. cummings, May Sarton and others; you may find them all in the index of authors and original languages. Today especially, as increasing numbers of people flee ecological, economic and political disasters, this collection my help us to look again at our values and collective history in order to focus on what we can do to improve the quality of human lives on our fragile planet.

A few of the quotations are from an earlier collection begun by my father, Will Taylor, in the 1920's, published in 1974 as *The Human Course: thoughts for living*. A philosopher and a psychologist, he was concerned with personal growth and responsibility to the community, education, history, love and death, and "the good life," well aware that traditional ideas have offered guidance throughout the ages for realizing the human potential, with respect for all members of society.

My mother, Phoebe Taylor, co-editor of *The Human Course*, initiated the first edition of *Thoughts...* (1987), with ideas on the importance of good communication and self-reliance— "the ultimate walking stick"— ideas strengthened after she became blind in 1962 and held steadfastly until her death in 1993. Unattributed quotations are hers.

These two shared the attributes of Sophocles, keeping an open mind, wary of complacency, ever ready to adapt to the changing circumstances of life's journey:

*A sailor has to tack and slacken sheets
Before the gale, or find himself capsized.*

This little book is offered in hopes that you will find here some inspiration for life's journey, bringing your own experience to bear on these ideas, as Schweizer believed we must do:

*Just as a tree bears year after year the same
fruit yet new, so must all valuable ideas be born
again in thought.*

                                    CTB, Santa Barbara, February 12, 1997

My life is nourished by the river,

And through its veins

The gifts of many mountain peaks run down;

Its fields grow richer from many rivers' silt!

The wondrous sap of life

Feeds the fields from many sources.

Its dream and its awakening

Are circled by many streams of songs

That flow from East and West.

Rabindranath Tagore, India, 1861-1941

I. FREE THOUGHT

Free and ranging thought begets the free spirit.

Even the night shall be light about me.   Psalm 139

Just as a tree bears

year after year

the same fruit yet new,

so must all valuable ideas

be born again in thought.

Albert Schweitzer, 1875-1965

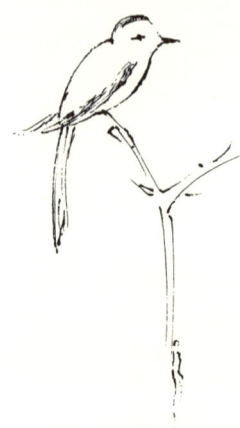

The swallow may be silent but never forgets its song.
It will sing it will cry out
when my country's olive trees blossom
when the sky's rains wash away
the spots of consumption and thorns of fate!

Mahmoud Darwish, 1942-
A Poem which is not green, from my country

With truth one goes everywhere, even in prison.

> Polish saying

Truth often loses by blind obedience,
but gains by inquiry.

> William Penn, 1644-1718

Ah! What a dusty answer gets the soul
When hot for certainties in this our life!

> George Meredith, 1828-1909

Knowledge is a wild thing and must be hunted
before it can be tamed.

> Persian saying

The complete skeptic will go nowhere, harboring
the delusion of futility.   Anon.

I learned by experiment, that if one advances confidently in the direction of his dreams and endeavors to live the life which he has imagined, he will meet with a success unexpected in common hours....In proportion as he simplifies his life, the laws of the universe will appear less complex, and solitude will not be solitude, nor poverty poverty, nor weakness weakness. If you have built castles in the air, your work need not be lost; it is where they should be. Now put the foundation under them.

* * *

Our village life would stagnate if it were not for the unexplored forests and meadows which surround it. We need the tonic of the wilderness....At the same time that we are earnest to explore and learn all things, we require that all things be mysterious and unexplorable, that land and sea be infinitely wild, unsurveyed and unfathomed by us because unfathomable.

Henry David Thoreau 1817-1862
A Week on the Concord and Merrimack Rivers

Where the mind is without fear and the head is held high;

Where knowledge is free;

Where the world has not been broken up into fragments

   by narrow domestic walls;

Where words come out from the depth of truth;

Where tireless striving stretches its arms towards

   perfection;

Where the clear stream of reason has not lost its way

   into the dreary desert sand of dead habit;

Where the mind is led forward—into ever-widening

   thought and action;

Into that heaven of freedom my Father let my country awake.

                          Rabindranath Tagore, India, 1861-1941

In our every deliberation, we must consider the impact of our decisions on the next seven generations.

> The Great Law of the six nations
> Iroquois confederacy

Great Spirit

Grant that I may not

Criticize my neighbor

Until I have walked a mile

In his moccasins

American Indian Saying

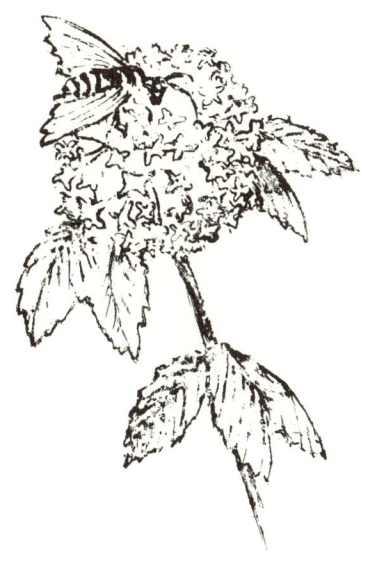

To make a prairie it takes a clover and one bee,

One clover, and a bee,

And revery.

The revery alone will do,

If bees are few.

                    Emily Dickinson, 1830-1886

Each time a man stands up for an ideal, or acts to improve the lot of others, or strikes out against injustice, he sends forth a tiny ripple of hope ... those ripples build a current which can sweep down the mightiest walls of oppression and resistance.

Robert Kennedy, 1925-1968

Remember that happiness can be only for the free, and that freedom is the sure possession of those alone who have the courage to defend it.

καὶ τὸ εὔδαιμον τὸ ἐλεύθερον,

τὸ δ'ἐλεύθερον τὸ εὔψυχον κρίναντες . . .

Pericles, 495?-429 B.C. Funeral oration on Athenians fallen in the Peloponnesian War.

When power leads man toward arrogance, poetry reminds him of his limitations. When power narrows the areas of man's concern, poetry reminds him of the richness and diversity of his existence. When power corrupts, poetry cleanses. For art establishes the basic human truth which must serve as the touchstone of our judgment.

John F. Kennedy, 1917-1963

Man is born with rainbows in his heart
And you'll never read him unless
You consider rainbows.

Carl Sandburg, 1878-1967

Gossip needs no carriage.

                        Russian proverb

Appear as thou art, or be as thou appearest.

                        Sufi teaching, Persia

The greatest disordering of the mind is believing
in things because one wants them to be.

*Le plus grand dérèglement de l'esprit est de
croire les choses parce qu'on veut qu'elles soient.*

                        Bossuet, 1627-1704

Reason leads to enlightenment,
Knowing that one does not know.   Anon.

Truth is the most valuable thing we have.
Let us economize it.

                        Mark Twain, 1835-1910

Earth might be fair and all men glad and wise.
Age after age their tragic empires rise,
Built while they dream, and in that dreaming weep;
Would Man but wake . . . .

                        Genevan Psalter

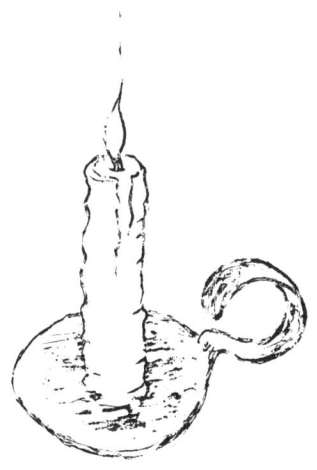

The old faiths light their candles all about;
But the burly Truth comes by and blows them out.

                Lizette W. Reese, 1856-1935

I know I own nothing
But the thought which unhindered
Will find its way from my soul,
And every favorable moment
That generous good fortune allows me
To fully enjoy.

Ich weiss, dass mir nichts angehört
Als der Gedanke, der ungestört
Aus meiner Seele will fliessen,
Und jeder günstige Augenblick,
Den mich ein Liebendes Geschick
Von Grund aus lässt geniessen.

Goethe 1749-1832

It is no weakness for the wisest man
To learn when he is wrong, know when to yield.
So, on the margin of a flooded river
Trees bending to the torrent live unbroken,
While those that strain against it are snapped off.
A sailor has to tack and slacken sheets
Before the gale, or find himself capsized . . . .
Let not your first thought be your only thought.
Think if there cannot be some other way.

                Sophocles, 5th century BC, *Antigone*

II. THE NATURAL WAY

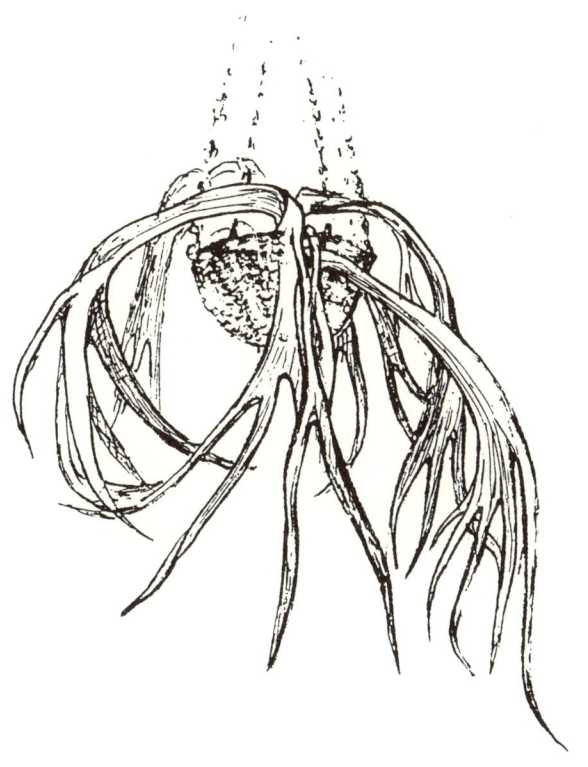

. . . to live on the fragrance of the earth

and like the air plant be sweetened by light.

Sherwood Anderson, 1876-1941

The native vision, the gift of seeing truly, with wonder and delight into the natural world, is informed by a certain attitude of reverence and respect. It is a matter of extrasensory as well as sensory perception. In addition to the eye, it involves the intelligence, the instinct, and the imagination. It is the perception not only of objects and forms but also of essences and ideals.

                              N. Scott Momaday, 1934-   Kiowa Indian

You whose day it is,

make it beautiful.

Get out your rainbow colors

so it will be beautiful.

Nootka Indian Song

to bring fair weather

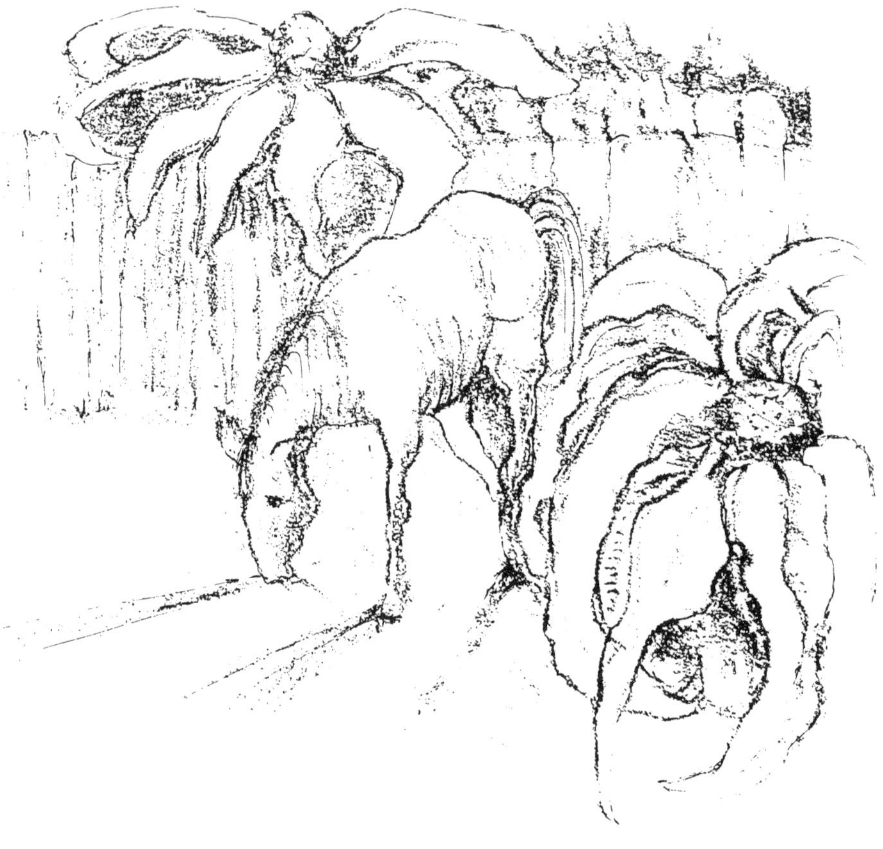

We are part fire and part dream

We are the physical mirroring

of Miaheyyun, the Total Universe

upon this earth, our Mother.

We are here to experience.

We are a movement of a hand

within millions of seasons,

a wink of touching

within millions and millions

of sun fires.

And we speak with the

Mirroring of the Sun.

The wind is the Spirit of these things.

Fire Dog, Cheyenne Indian

The world is too much with us: late and soon,
Getting and spending, we lay waste our powers.
Little we see in Nature that is ours;
We have given our hearts away, a sordid boon!
The sea that bares her bosom to the moon;
The winds that will be howling at all hours,
And are up-gathered now like sleeping flowers;
For this, for everything, we are out of tune;
It moves us not. —Great God! I'd rather be
A pagan suckled in a creed outworn.
So might I, standing on this pleasant lea,
Have glimpses that would make me less forlorn;
Have sight of Proteus rising from the sea;
Or hear old Triton blow his wreathed horn.

William Wordsworth, 1770-1850

I sometimes wonder if the absence of thought, and the absence of morality, do not contribute largely to the great dignity of the beasts, the plants and the waters.

J'hésite parfois si l'absence de pensée, et l'absence de morale, ne contribuent pas beaucoup à la grande dignité des bêtes, des plantes et des eaux.

Henri de Montherlant, 1896-1972

In small proportion we just beauties see,
And in short measures, life may perfect be.

      Ben Jonson, 1573-1637

The days grow long, the mountains
Beautiful. The south wind blows
Over blossoming meadows.
Newly arrived swallows dart
Over the steaming marshes.
Ducks in pairs drowse on warm sand.

    Tu Fu, 8th c. *South Wind*

The earth has drunk the snow,
The plum trees are blossoming once more.
The willow leaves are like new gold;
The lake is molten silver.
It is the hour of
Sulphur-laden butterflies,
Velvet heads upon the flowers.

The fisherman casts forth his nets
From an unmoving boat,
The surface of the lake is broken.
His thoughts are at home with her
To whom he will return with food,
Like a swallow to its mate.

    Li Po, 8th c. *The Fisherman*

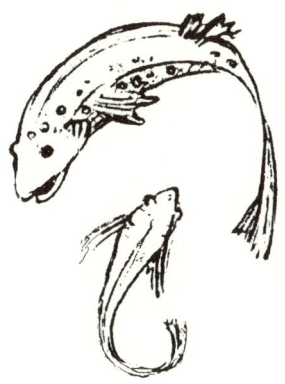

A trout leaps high—
In the river beneath him
Clouds drift by.

Onitsura, 17-18 c.

The lark . . .
Rises and begins to round,
He drops the silver chain of sound,
Of many links without a break,
In chirrup, whistle, slur and shake,
All intervolved and spreading wide,
Like water-dimples down a tide
Where ripple ripple overcurls
And eddy into eddy whirls . . . .
But wider over many heads
The starry voice ascending spreads,
Awakening, as it waxes thin,
The best in us to him akin . . . .

For singing till his heaven fills,
'Tis love of earth that he instils,
And ever winging up and up,
Our valley is his golden cup;

And he the wine which overflows
To lift us with him as he goes,
The woods and brooks, the sheep and kine,
He is, the hills, the human line,
The meadows green, the fallows brown,
The dreams of labor in the town;
He sings the sap, the quickened veins,
The wedding song of sun and rains
He is, the dance of children, thanks
Of sowers, shout of primrose-banks,
And eye of violets while they breathe;
All these the circling song will wreathe,
And you shall hear the herb and tree,
The better heart of men shall see,
Shall feel celestially, as long
As you crave nothing save the song.

George Meredith 1828-1909

> Inebriate of air am I,
> And debauchée of dew.

>> Emily Dickinson, 1830-1886

> On certain mornings, as we turn a corner, an exquisite dew falls on our heart and then vanishes. But the freshness lingers, and this, always, is what the heart needs. The earth must have risen in just such a light the morning the world was born.

>> Albert Camus, 1913-1960

Life is tall lilacs all giddy with dew.

Peter Viereck, 1916-

June shall scatter May.

These I have loved . . .
Wet roofs, beneath the lamp-light; the strong crust
Of friendly bread; and many tasting food;
Rainbows; and the blue bitter smoke of wood;
And radiant raindrops couching in cool flowers;
And flowers themselves, that sway through sunny hours,
Dreaming of moths that drink them under the moon . . .

The benison of hot water; furs to touch;
The good smell of old clothes; and other such . . . .
Hair's fragrance, and the musty reek that lingers
About dead leaves and last year's ferns . . . .

Sweet water's dimpling laugh from tap or spring;
Holes in the ground; and voices that do sing;
Voices in laughter, too; and body's pain,
Soon turned to peace; and the deep-panting train;
Firm sands; the little dulling edge of foam
That browns and dwindles as the wave goes home;
And washen stones, gay for an hour; the cold
Graveness of iron; moist black earthen mould;
Sleep; and high places; footprints in the dew;
And oaks; and brown horse-chestnuts, glossy-new;
And new-peeled sticks; and shining pools on grass; —
All these have been my loves . . . .

                    Rupert Brooke   1887-1915   *The Great Lover*

We have found safety with all things undying,
The winds, and morning, tears of men and mirth,
The deep night, and birds singing, and clouds flying,
And sleep, and freedom, and the autumnal earth . . . .

        Rupert Brooke, 1887-1915 *Safety*

And Life is Colour and Warmth and Light,
And a striving . . . .

        Julian Grenfell, 1888-1915

With a feast spread in springtime,

A cup of green wine and a joyous song,

I repeat my salutation and offer three wishes:

First, may you have a long life;

Second, may I have good health;

Third, may we live like swallows on the beam,

Happily together all the year round.

Feng Yen-Chi, 10th c. *Her Birthday*

XIV

In their assault on the gardens
The seasons are everywhere at once
The passion of summer for winter
And the tenderness of the other two
Memories like feathers
The trees have shattered the sky
A fine oak spoiled by the fog
The life of the birds or the life of feathers
And the whole frivolous panache
With smiling fears
And gossiping solitude.

XIV

A l'assaut des jardins
Les saisons sont partout à la fois
Passion de l'été pour l'hiver
Et la tendresse des deux autres
Les souvenirs comme des plumes
Les arbres ont brisé le ciel
Un beau chêne gâché de brume
La vie des oiseaux ou la vie des plumes
Et tout un panache frivole
Avec de souriantes craintes
Et la solitude bavarde.

Paul Eluard, 1895-1952, *L'Amour la poésie*

yes is a pleasant country:
if's wintry
(my lovely)
let's open the year

both is the very weather
(not either)
my treasure,
when violets appear

love is a deeper season
than reason;
my sweet one
(and april's where we're)

                    ee cummings, 1894-1962
                    XXXVIII in 1X1

life is more true than reason will deceive
(more secret or than madness did reveal)
deeper is life than lose: higher than have
—but beauty is more each than living's all

multiplied with infinity sans if
the mightiest meditations of mankind
cancelled are by one merely opening leaf
(beyond whose nearness there is no beyond)

or does some littler bird than eyes can learn
look up to silence and completely sing?
futures are obsolete; pasts are unborn
(here less than nothing's more than everything)

death, as men call him, ends what they call men
—but beauty is more now than dying's when

                ee cummings, 1894-1962
                LII in 1X1

III. LIFE IN TIME

To see a World in a Grain of Sand
And a Heaven in a Wild Flower
Hold Infinity in the palm of your hand
And Eternity in an hour...

> William Blake 1757-1827
> *Auguries of Innocence*

The way to do is to be.

> Lao Tsu, 6th century B.C.

That which oft holds back the tears in my weeping eye
Is a child at play or a bird in flight.

*Was im weinenden Auge mir oft die Tränen zurückhält,
Ist ein spielendes Kind oder ein Vogel im Flug.*

     Justinus Kerner, 1786-1862

There is a song sleeping in all things
That dream on and on,
And the world will awaken to sing
If only you can find the magic word.

*Schläft ein Lied in allen Dingen,
Die da traumen fort und fort,
Und die Welt hebt an zu singen
Triffst du nur das Zauberwort.*

   Joseph Freiherr von Eichendorff, 1788-1857

I cannot be sure of the paper rose,
however many times I made it with my hands!
Nor do I put my faith in the other, true rose,
daughter of the sun and season,
betrothed to the wind.
In you, whom I never made,
in you, whom nobody ever made,
I put my trust, round and certain chance.

No me fío de la rosa
de papel,
tantas veces que la hice
yo con mis manos!
Ni me fío de la otra
rosa verdadera,
hija del sol y sazón,
la prometida del viento.
De ti, que nunca te hice,
de ti, que nunca te hicieron,
de ti me fío, redondo
seguro azar.

Pedro Salinas, 1891-1951, "Fe mia", 1929

Enjoy the world gently,

Enjoy the world gently,

If the world is spoilt,

No one can repair it,

Enjoy the world gently.

Yoruba song

When you drink the water, think of the spring.
Czech saying

When you drink the water, think of the well digger.
Russian saying

Land belongs to a large family of man
some of whom are dead, many of whom are
living, and most of whom are yet unborn.

Nigerian Chief

Respect and love sustain each other.

To have heard the jade growing in the cliff.

Lao Tsu, Sixth century B.C.

Love's mysteries in souls do grow
But yet the body is his book.

John Donne, 1572-1631 *The Ecstasy*

Love and smoke are two things which can't be concealed.

Old French Proverb

Love is fostered by confidence and constancy; one
who is able to give much is also able to love much.

Propertius b. ca. 51 B.C. *Elegies*

Love withers under constraint; its very essence is liberty; it is compatible neither with obedience, jealousy, nor fear; it is there most pure, perfect, and unlimited where its votaries live in confidence, equality, and unreserve.

Percy Bysshe Shelley 1792-1822

Life is a pure flame, and we live by an invisible sun within us.

        Sir Thomas Browne, 1605-1682

Our lives shall be variable as the shade
the quivering aspens made.

        Sir Walter Scott, 1771-1832

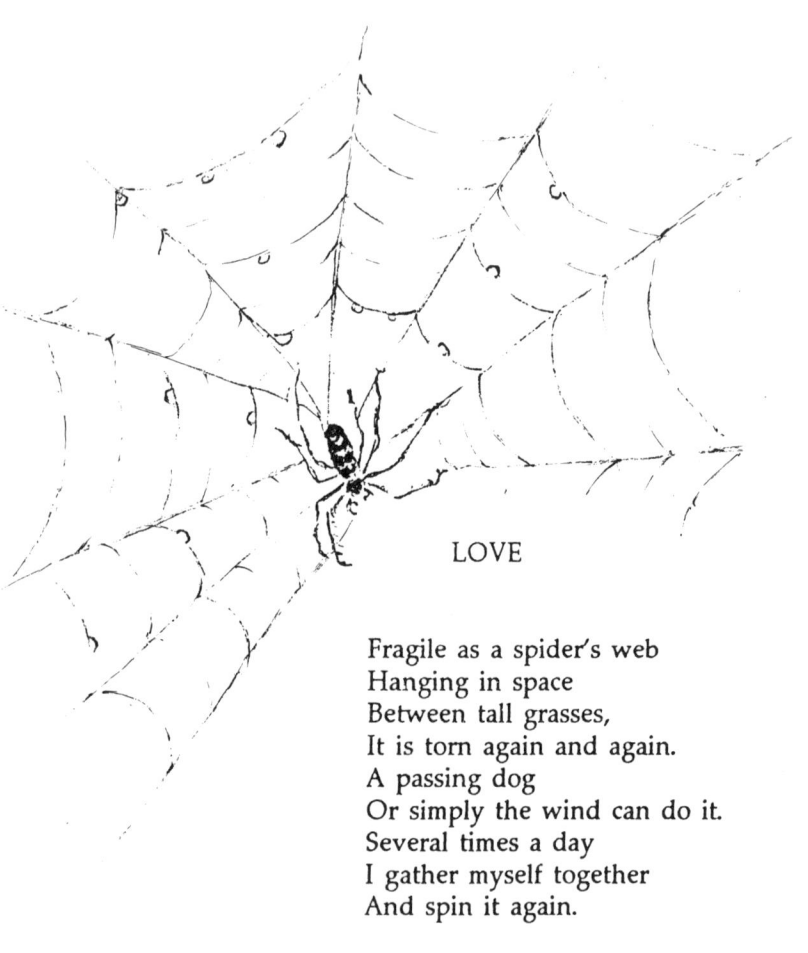

LOVE

Fragile as a spider's web
Hanging in space
Between tall grasses,
It is torn again and again.
A passing dog
Or simply the wind can do it.
Several times a day
I gather myself together
And spin it again.

Spiders are patient weavers.
They never give up.
And who knows
What keeps them at it?
Hunger, no doubt,
And hope.

May Sarton, 1912-1995

OF MOLLUSCS

As the tide rises, the closed mollusc
Opens a fraction to the ocean's food,
Bathed in its riches. Do not ask
What force would do, or if force could.

A knife is of no use against a fortress
You might break it to pieces as gulls do.
No, only the rising tide and its slow progress
Opens the shell. Lovers, I tell you true.

You who have held yourselves closed hard
Against warm sun and wind, shelled up in fears
And hostile to the touch or a tender word
The ocean rises, salt as unshed tears.

Now you are floated on this gentle flood
That cannot force or be forced, welcome food
Salt as your tears, the ocean's blood
Eat, rest, be nourished on the tide of love.

       May Sarton 1912-1995
       in *Halfway to Silence*, 1980

The seed ye sow, another reaps;
The wealth ye find, another keeps;
The robe ye weave, another wears;
The arms ye forge, another bears.

        Shelley, "Song to the men of England"

Hate blows a bubble of despair into
hugeness world system universe and BANG
— fear buries a tomorrow under woe
and up comes yesterday most green and young

pleasure and pain are merely surfaces
(one itself showing, itself hiding one)
life's only true value neither is
love makes the little thickness of the coin.
. . . .

        e e cummings, 1894-1962
        50 poems (1940)

Friendship draws men together,
self-interest separates them.

> The Talmud

Hatred is like rain in a desert —-
it is of no use to anybody.

> Yoruba saying

The biting fly gets nothing by alighting
on the back of the tortoise.

Ohurii si akyekyere akyi keva.

The biting fly has no one
To come to his aid in trouble.

Ohurii nni gyamfo.

> Ashanti Proverbs, Gold Coast

bright doors, an empty mansion, no one living there
and in the village hall the happiest of plowmen
an instant and both wealth and rank are empty blossoms
leaves flown on autumn wind and ragged rain

nothing would be better than to see you again
to sail in a little boat
to wait the plums that bloom in snow and frost
wander together
beside the shallows of cold pools

> Feng Tzu-Chen, *Brief Dreams of Glory* in *The Wine of Endless Life: Taoist Drinking Songs of the Yuan Dynasty.* Translated by Jerome B. Seaton

Life is like the moon;
Now dark, now full.

                        Polish proverb

Time has many a night and day to run
On his uncounted course; in one of these
Some little rift will come, and the sword's point
Will make short work of this day's harmony.

                    μυρίας ὁ μύριος
     χρόνος τεκνοῦται νύκτας ἡμέρας τ' ἰών,
     ἐν αἷς τὰ νῦν ξύμφωνα δεξιώματα
     δόρει διασκεδῶσιν ἐκ σμικροῦ λόγου·

      Sophocles, 496-406 B.C. *Oedipus at Colonus*

The morning stars sang together . . . .

                Book of Job 38.7

. . . scattering a path of golden dust along life's way.

                Gustave Flaubert, 1821-1880

Canst thou bind the sweet influence of Pleaides,
Or loose the bands of Orion?

Book of Job, 38.31

What's to come is still unsure.
Youth's a stuff will not endure.

Shakespeare, 1564-1616

That is the land of lost content,
I see it shining plain,
The happy highways where I went
And cannot come again.

A. E. Housman, 1859-1936

UNIDAD

Hay algo denso, unido, sentado en el fondo,
repitiendo su número, su señal idéntica.
Cómo se nota que las piedras han tocado el tiempo,
en su fina materia hay olor a edad
y el agua que trae el mar, de sal y sueño.

Me rodea una misma cosa, un solo movimiento:
el peso del mineral, la luz de la piel,
se pegan al sonido de la palabra noche:
la tinta del trigo, del marfil, del llanto,
las cosas de cuero, de madera, de lana,
envejecidas, desteñidas, uniformes,
se unen en torno a mí como paredes.

Trabajo sordamente, girando sobre mí mismo,
como el cuervo sobre la muerte, el cuervo de luto.
Pienso, aislado en lo extremo de las estaciones,
central, rodeado de geografía silenciosa:
una temperatura parcial cae del cielo,
un extremo imperio de confusas unidades
se reúne rodeándome.

Pablo Neruda

UNITY

There is something dense, united, founded in the depths,
repeating its number, its identical sign.
It is apparent that the rock has touched time,
in its fine substance there is the scent of age
and of the water of salt and dreams the sea brings.

A single thing circles round me, a single movement:
the weight of mineral, the glow of skin
cling to the sound of the word "night":
the shades of wheat, of marble, of weeping,
of leather, wooden, woolly things,
aging, faded, or uniform,
come together like walls around me.

I work without a sound, circling over myself,
like the crow of mourning over death. Isolated
in the extreme of the seasons, I reflect,
central, surrounded by a silent geography:
a partial temperature descends from the sky,
an ultimate empire of mingled unities
comes together around me.

      Pablo Neruda, 1904-1973, Chile

We have only to look around us, at the fissures in the rock-wall of our times, to know that we have created for ourselves a madhouse of irrationality and despair. The lunacies of our world erupt daily like boils on the diseased body of civilization. Is it, hopefully, the reawakening of conscience, or, more likely, the refracted pain of denying our souls?

Alienation....The explanation for racial strife, random violence, mass madness, the rape of our planet. Man feels cut off. He feels denied. He feels alone....Alone against his world, the man of today finds his gods have deserted him, his brother has grown fangs, the machine clatters ever nearer on his heels, fear is the only lover demanding his clasp....

The creative intellect struggles against the shuddering membrane of alienation, against the interface between himself and freedom of the soul, the artist tries to gain an exit with the magics of words and movements and colors. Yet all around him the inexorable inertia of the alienated society finds the strength to keep rolling, grinding, crushing....

>Harlan Ellison, from the introduction
>to *Alone Against Tomorrow*, 1971

Bear not the burden of a world outworn,
Nor to the future bow;
With every hour thy joy be newly born,
And earth be new-created every morn --
Thy life is here and now.

    Bhartrihari, 7th century, India

Time hath nor enemy nor friend . . .
Like as the Wind upon the field
Bow every herb, and all must yield . . .
We beneath Time's passing breath
Bow each in turn, -- why tears for birth or death?

    Bhartrihari. Translated from the Sanskrit
    by Paul Elmer More, 1864-1937

Thou art indeed just, Lord, if I contend
With thee; (but, sir, so what I plead is just.)
Why do sinners' ways prosper? and why must
Disappointment all I endeavor end?
Wert thou my enemy, O thou my friend,
How wouldst thou worse, I wonder, than thou dost
Defeat, thwart me? O the sots and thralls of lust
Do in spare hours more thrive than I that spend,
Sir, life upon thy cause. See, banks and brakes
Now, leaved how thick! laced they are again
With fretty chervil, look, and fresh wind shakes
Them; birds build—but not I build; no, but strain,
Time's eunuch, and not breed one work that wakes
Mine, O thou lord of life, send my roots rain.

                Gerard Manley Hopkins, 1844-1889

How arrives it joy lies slain,
And why unblooms the best hope ever sown?
Crass Casualty obstructs the sun and rain,
And dicing Time for gladness casts a moan.
The purblind Doomsters had as readily strown
Blisses about my pilgrimage as pain.

                Thomas Hardy, 1840-1828

*Tristes guerras
si no es amor la empresa.
Tristes, tristes.*

*Tristes armas
si no son las palabras.
Tristes, tristes.*

*Tristes hombres
si no mueren de amores.
Tristes, tristes.*

    Miguel Hernandez, 1910-1942

Sad are wars that are not fought for love;
sad are the weapons when they are not words;
sad are the men who do not die for love.

The night of autumn travels with seven horses.
                              Finnish proverb

Youth is a garland of roses,
Old age a garland of willows.   Aramaic saying

What I aspired to be,
And was not, comforts me.
                    Robert Browning, 1812-1889
                         Rabbi Ben Ezra

Where I sought shade in soul, a gnarled
old cactus was scornfully growing.   P.T.

In the beauty of the garden, the mind turns . . .
all that's made to a green thought in a green shade.

                         Andrew Marvell, 1621-1678

The wind is my refuge, the opposite shore my support.
Who lies down when the wind is fair must row
when the wind is against him.

What the waterfall brings the stream carries away.

Finnish proverbs

An aged man is but a paltry thing,
A tattered coat upon a stick, unless
Soul clap its hands and sing,
       and louder sing,
For every tatter in its mortal dress . . . .

W. B. Yeats, 1865-1939

For they hear the wind laugh, and murmur and sing
Of a land where even the old are fair,
And even the wise are merry of tongue,
But I heard a reed of Coolaney say,
'When the wind has laughed and murmured and sung,
The lonely of heart is withered away.'

English folklore

Pleasures are like poppies spread,
You seize the flowers, its bloom is shed;
Or like the snow-fall in the river,
A moment white, then melts forever.

                      Robert Burns, 1756-1796

Does disappointment or loss raise your sights to reason,
or do you lose yourself to the "poppied warmth" of sleep?

Sleep is . . . sore labor's bath,
Balm of hurt minds, great Nature's second course.

                      Shakespeare, *Macbeth*

LOS ENIGMAS

*Me habéis preguntado qué hila el crustaceo
entre sus patas de oro
y os respondo: El mar lo sabe....*

You have asked me, what is the lobster weaving
  between his golden feet?
I reply, the ocean knows.
You say, what is the ascidia waiting for in its
  transparent bell? What is it waiting for?
I tell you it waits for time, as you do.
You inquire, whom does the Macrocystis alga embrace?
Look around, at a certain hour, in a certain sea I know.

You will ask about the accursed ivory tusk of the narwhale
  so I may tell you how the harpooned sea unicorn dies.
And you inquire, what of the kingfisher feathers fluttering
  in the pure waters of the southern tides?
Have you shuffled the cards and dealt out one more question
  on the limpid structure of the polyp?

Must you know about the electric matter of the spiny depths?
  The armored stalactite that breaks while walking?
  The hook of the angler fish? music reaching
    like a thread through the depths?

I tell you, the ocean knows this, the life in its
  coffers is vast like the pure sands, and among
the blood-red grapes of the vine, time has polished
the petals, made the light of the jelly fish,
    and plucked coral strands from their branch
      in a horn of plenty made of infinite mother of pearl.

I am only the empty net which goes ahead of
human eyes, lifeless in those half-lights,
fingers accustomed to the triangle,
the measures of an orange's shy hemisphere.

I walked around as you do, investigating
the endless star, and at night
I awoke naked in my net, the only thing caught,
a fish trapped in the wind.

                      Pablo Neruda, 1904-1973, Chile

There is a budding morrow in midnight.

John Keats, 1795-1821

O weep no more;
Young buds sleep in the root's white core.

Shelley, 1792-1822

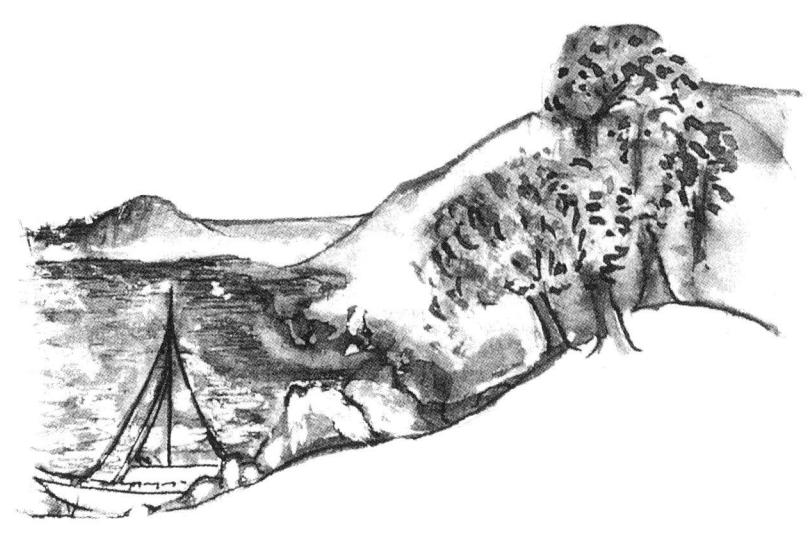

A shipwrecked sailor buried on this coast
Bids you set sail
Full many a bark, when we were lost,
Weathered the gale.

                                          Greek epitaph

IV. ART OF LIVING

los animos descompuestos

y alivia los trabajos

del espiritu.

Music restores order to our spirits

and lightens the concerns of the mind.

Cervantes 1547-1616

The magic of music is in its effect on volition. A sudden clearing of the mind of rubbish and the reestablishment of a sense of proportion.

> Ezra Pound, 1885-1972
> *Guide to Kulchur*

I did not set out to design a house that hung from a pole, or to manufacture a new type of automobile, invent a new system of map projection, develop geodesic domes or Energetic-Synergetic geometry. I started with the universe—as an organization of energy systems of which all our experiences...are only local instances.

I could have ended up with a pair of flying slippers.

> R. Buckminster Fuller 1895-1983

Every child is an artist. The problem is how to remain an artist once he grows up.

> Pablo Picasso   1881-1973

As in art, so in human ways, balance
and proportion lead to sweetness and light.
Good taste is the flower of good sense . . .
inwardly clear, outwardly fit.

We are born sleeping and few of us ever awake, unless it is when death startles us and we learn what bit of Olympian fire our humid forms enwrapped. But we could open our eyes to joy also. The artist cries "Awake!" and sings the song of the morning.

This is the priesthood of art—not to bestow upon the universe a new aspect, but upon the beholder a new enthusiasm.

Max Eastman, 1883-1969

Like the balsam, scarred but upright, in the dignity of accepting loss, one can still be free.

Only with self-respect can we be truly kind, with sympathy and understanding for those with whom we disagree.

There are some trips to be taken alone. No companion can be as steadfast as Self-reliance, the supreme walking-stick.

To be only "tolerant" is less than to be kind.

Be candid to admit failure, courageous to mock it.

P.T.

If a way to the better there be,
It exacts a full look at the worst.

                Thomas Hardy, 1840-1928

Your fame is no more than a sunlit day.

Instabile sereno è vostra fama . . . .

                Petrarch, 1304-1374, *Triumphus Temporis*

Unstable as the water, thou shalt not excel.

                Genesis 49.4

Today well lived

Makes every yesterday a dream of happiness

And every tomorrow a vision of hope.

                                          Sanskrit teaching

Upon an everlasting tide
Into the silent seas we go;
But verdure laughs along the side,
And roses on the margin blow.

Nor life, nor death, nor aught they hold,
Rate thou above their natural height;
Yet learn that all our eyes behold
Has value, if we mete it right.

Pluck then the flowers that line the stream,
Instead of fighting with its power;
But pluck as flowers, not gems, nor deem
That they will bloom beyond their hour.

What e're betides, from day to day,
An even pulse and spirit keep;
And like a child, worn out with play,
When wearied with existence, sleep.

Francis Hastings Doyle, 1810-1888

Only among the open-minded does true conversation
prevail; a dogmatist cannot know true dialogue.

The better to persuade, clothe weighty ideas in motley.

A balm for the fretted soul, let whimsey and humor
displace annoyance. Let mirth follow in your wake.   P.T.

It is to a man's honor to avoid strife, but every fool
is quick to quarrel.

The purposes of another's heart are deep waters,
but one of understanding draws them out.

Proverbs 20:3-5

Pleasant words are sweet to the soul.   Proverbs XVI

Swearing is the poor man's poetry.   Anon.

> If of thy mortal goods thou art bereft,
> And from thy slender store two loaves
>   alone to thee are left,
> Sell one, and with the dole
> Buy hyacinths to feed thy soul.

Saadi, 1184-1291   Persian

Loafing invites the soul.

Lessen your wants . . .

husband your powers . . . . Fewer
strokes can make a more powerful image.

        Lao Tsu, Sixth century B.C.

Beloved Pan, and all ye gods that haunt this place, make me beautiful within; and may the outward and inward man be at one. May I count the wise to be wealthy, and may I have only such goods as a temperate man, and he alone, can use and support.

                        Socrates, ca. 470-399 B.C.

A man is rich in proportion to the number of things he can afford to let alone.

                        Henry David Thoreau, 1817-1862

I learn by going where I have to go.

> Theodore Roethke   1908-1963

Traveler, the path is just your footprints,
nothing more; making our way, there is no
ready-made path, we make it as we go along.

> *Caminante, son tus huellas*
> *el camino, y nada más;*
> *caminante, no hay camino,*
> *se hace camino al andar.*

> Antonio Machado   1875-1939

What one does, one becomes.

> Japanese proverb

Habit is but long practice, friend,
And this becomes men's nature in the end.

> Aristotle,   *Nicomachean Ethics VIIx*

Silence speaks louder than words.
Yet oft by silence error is approved.　　Anon.

Compassion is a kind of alchemy to restore the soul.

Be to her virtues kind,
To her faults a little blind.

When wilt thou learn that to be swift is less sure
than to be wise, and pleasure may be lost?
Pause, then, to sniff a rose.

Seek not what makes you gyrate,
but what makes you dance.　　P.T.

A glass of milk, a ham on rye and thou . . . .

    Pursue, keep up with, circle round and round your life, as a dog does his master's chaise. Do what you love.
    Know your own bone, gnaw at it, bury it, unearth it, and gnaw it still.

Henry David Thoreau, 1817-1862

Let us reason together . . . .   Isaiah I 18

The tongue of the wise is in his heart,
The heart of the fool is in his mouth.

>   Arabic saying

The tongue kills man and the tongue saves man.
He who is dishonest with respect to speech
is dishonest in everything.

>   Ashanti sayings

Who will dance to a lion's roaring?

>   Swahili saying

The more you lament the more is your loss.

>   Persian proverb

Pleasures were cheap before money became dear.

> Czech saying

To bend in a place is to rise in that place.

> Swahili proverb

It's better to return from half-way
than to lose your way.

> Hungarian proverb

A clever man turns great troubles into little ones,
the little ones into none at all.

> Czech proverb

To the Thawing Wind

Come with rain, O loud Southwester!
Bring the singer; bring the nester;
Give the buried flower a dream;
Make the settled snow-bank stream;
Find the brown beneath the white;
But whate'er you do tonight,
Bathe my window, make it flow,
Melt it as the ice will go;
Melt the glass and leave the sticks
Like a hermit's crucifix;
Burst into my narrow stall;
Swing the picture on the wall;
Run the rattling pages o'er;
Scatter poems on the floor;
Turn the poet out of door.

Robert Frost 1874-1963
in *A Boy's Will*, 1913

The best way of living is like water.
Water benefits everything and does not strive.
It dwells in places men do not value . . . .
In dwelling, one may adapt to the surroundings.
In meditation, one may go deep.
In dealing with others, one may be gentle and kind.
In speech, do and say what you mean.
In ruling, one can be fair in control and rule well.
In business, be competent.
In action, be timely.

No fight: no blame.

        Lao Tsu, *Tao Te Ching, VIII*   6th century BC

To talk little is natural.
High winds do not last all morning.
Heavy rain won't last all day.
Why is it so? Heaven and earth!

If heaven and earth cannot be eternal,
How is it possible for man?

One who follows the natural way
Is at one with the way.
He who is a virtuous person
Experiences virtue.
He who loses the way feels lost . . . .

When you are at one with Virtue,
Virtue is always there.
When you are at one with loss
The loss is experienced willingly.

One who does not trust enough
May not be trusted.

Lao Tsu, *Tao Te Ching, XXIII* 6th century BC

'Tis better to write of laughter than of tears,
For laughter is natural to man.

Mieulx est de ris que de larmes escrire,
Pource que rire est le propre de l'homme.

Rabelais, 1490-1553   *Aux Lecteurs*

Don't sweat the small stuff. It's all small stuff.
If you can't fight and you can't flee, flow.

Cardiologist, U. Nebraska, 1982

Oh children, rain of the spring, buds of hope!

يا ايها الاطفال ...
يا مطر الربيع
يا سنابل الآمال ...

                    Nizar Qabbani, 1923-

Ah bring back to me
the star-charts of childhood
that I may share
with the young swallows
the road of return
to the nest of your expectations!

                Mahmud Darwish 1942- *To my Mother*

We can help make the world safe for diversity
For in the final analysis our most basic common link
   is that we all inhabit this small planet . . . .
We all breathe the same air,
We all cherish our children's future
And we are all mortal.

                John F. Kennedy 1917-1963

V. OUT OF TIME

Behold, in yon stripped Autumn, in shivering grey,
Earth knows no desolation.
She smells generation
In the moist breath of decay.

        George Meredith, 1828-1909

Nee man can tether Time nor Tide.

Robert Burns 1756-1796

Those hours that with gentle work did frame
The lovely gaze where every eye doth dwell
Will play the tyrants to the very same
And that unfair which fairly doth excel:

For never-resting time leads summer on
To hideous winter and confounds him there,
Sap check'd with frost and lusty leaves quite gone,
Beauty o'ersnow'd and bareness everywhere.

Then, were not summer's distillation left,
A liquid prisoner pent in walls of glass,
Beauty's effect with beauty were bereft,
Nor it, nor no remembrance what it was:

But flowers distill'd, though they with winter meet,
Lose but their show; their substance still lives sweet.

       Shakespeare, 1564-1616 Sonnet V

    Lu Tung-Pin is
              gone beyond
    his spirit suns
    a thousand other worlds
    merit, fame, and grass and mustard seed
    the same
    the old guy took his bramble staff
    and smashed up all
              distinctions.

    no tricks
            nothing doing.
    sun and moon endure their rush
    and don't grow old.
    sail backwards?
    row against the flow?
    to hell with that.
    you'd better be known
    for being
            quiet.

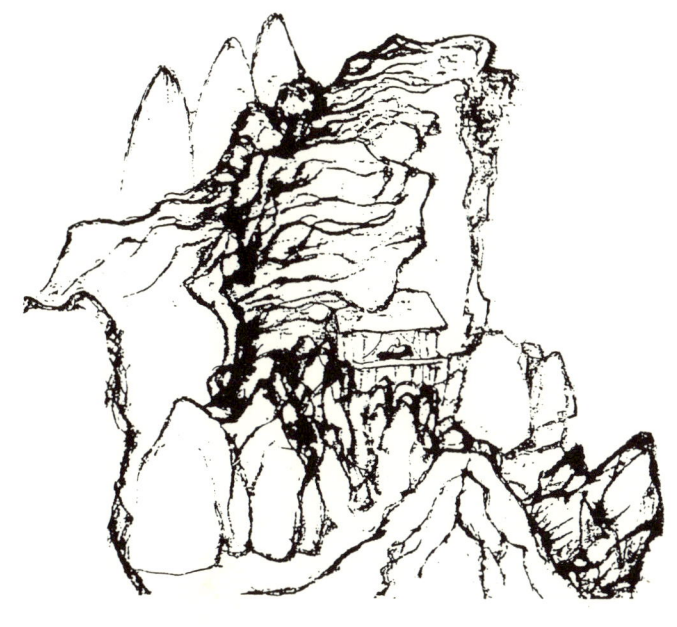

clear water-sound
fine mountain colors
nothing to do
    with right and wrong
bamboo's shade on a
rush hut's window
here's music
in a way
you cannot say
to any man

                    Yün K'an Tzu, Yüan Dynasty

Bards of Passion and of Mirth,

Ye have left your souls on Earth!

John Keats, 1795-1821

Each of us suffers his own peculiar ghost.
But the day comes when we are sent through wide Elysium,
The field of the Blessed, a few of us, to linger
Until the turn of Time, the wheel of the ages,
Wears off the taint, and leaves the core of spirit
Pure sense, pure flame.

Quisque suos patimur manis: exinde per amplum
Mittimur Elysium et pauci laeta arva tenemus,
Donec longo dies, perfecto temporis orbe,
Concretam exemit labem purumque relinquit.
Aetherium sensum atque aurai simplicis ignem.

Virgil, 70-19 B.C. *Aeneid*

Who will know my name?

    at least my songs?

    at least my flowers?

    What is there to do?

Are we here on earth for nothing?

    at least my songs

    at least my flowers

    Aztec, Nahuatl song

Heaven trims our lamps while we sleep.

                A. Bronson Alcott, 1799-1888

No single thing abides, but all things flow.
Even the systems and their suns shall go back
Slowly to the eternal drift.

                Lucretius, 96-55 B.C.   *De Rerum Natura*

Above the chorus,
Listen! A single cricket
shakes a golden bell.

Kyoshi, Japanese, 1874-1959

世の中に
金鈴ろろろ
虫一つ

盧子

INDEX OF ORIGINAL LANGUAGES
other than English

American Indian	15
Cheyenne	29
Iroquois	15
Kiowa	26
Nahuatl (Aztec)	103
Nootka	27
Arabic	10, 89, 95
Aramaic	66
Ashanti (Gold Coast)	55, 89
Bengali (India)	5, 13
Chinese	32, 45, 49, 56, 84, 92, 102
Czech	48, 90
Finnish	66, 67
French	20, 31, 36, 41, 50, 58, 94
Greek	18, 23, 56, 73, 85, 86
Hebrew	7, 55, 58, 73, 76, 79, 83, 89
Hungarian	90
Indian	63
Italian	79
Japanese	33, 86, 105
Latin	21, 50, 79, 104
Persian	11, 20, 83, 89
Polish	11, 56
Russian	20, 48
Sanskrit	63, 80
Spanish	7, 60, 65, 70, 75, 86
Swahili	89, 90
Yoruba (Nigeria)	48, 55

INDEX OF AUTHORS

Alcott, A. Bronson	104	Blake, William	45
Anderson, Sherwood	25	Brooke, Rupert	38, 39
Aristotle	86	Browne, Sir Thomas	51
Bhartrihari	63	Browning, Robert	66

Burns, Robert	69, 98	Momaday, N. Scott	26
Camus, Albert	36	Montherlant	31
Cervantes	75	Neruda, Pablo	60, 70
cummings, e.e.	42, 43, 54	Onitsura	33
Darwish, Mahmud	10, 95	Penn, William	11
Dickinson, Emily	17, 36	Petrarch	79
Donne, John	50	Pericles	18
Doyle, Francis Hastings	81	Picasso, Pablo	76
Eastman, Max	77	Pound, Ezra	76
Ellison, Harlan	62	Propertius	48
Eluard, Paul	41	Proverbs	82
Feng Yen-Chi	40	Psalm 139	7
Feng Tzu-Chen	56	Qabbani, Nizar	95
Flaubert, Gustave	58	Rabelais, François	94
Frost, Robert	iv, 91	Reese, Lizette	21
Fuller, R. Buckminster	76	Roethke, Theodore	86
Genesis	79	Saadi	83
Goethe, Wolfgang	22	Salinas, Pedro	47
Grenfell, Julian	39	Sandburg, Carl	19
Hardy, Thomas	64, 79	Sarton, May	52, 53
Hernandez, Miguel	65	Schweitzer, Albert	9
Hopkins, Gerard Manley	64	Scott, Sir Walter	51
Housman, A. E.	59	Shakespeare	1, 57, 59, 99
Isaiah	89	Shelley, Percy B.	50, 54, 72
Job 38.7, 38.31	58, 59	Socrates	85
Jonson, Ben	32	Sophocles	23, 57
Keats, John	72, 102	Taylor, Phoebe	78, 82
Kennedy, John F.	19, 95	Tagore, Rabindranath	5, 13
Kennedy, Robert	18	Thoreau	12, 82, 85, 88
Kerner, Justinus	46	Tu Fu	32
Kyoshi	105	Twain, Mark	20
Lao Tsu	45, 49, 84, 92, 93	Viereck, Peter	37
Li Po	32	Virgil	102
Lucretius	104	Von Eichendorff, J.F.	46
Machado, Antonio	86	Wordsworth, William	30
Marvell, Andrew	66	Yeats, W.B.	68
Meredith, George	11, 34, 97	Yün K'an Tzu	100